GW00371835

PAST and PRESENT

No 8

FRONT COVER:
UFFCULME: The Culm Valley Light Railway opened on 29 May 1876 and ran for some $7^1/2$ miles through picturesque farming country. The route followed the course of the River Culm closely which enabled construction costs to be kept to a minimum, but the lightly laid and sharply curving track limited both the engines and stock that could be used. On 3 November 1962, 0-4-2T No 1421 leaves the village of Uffculme with the 12.09 pm Culmstock–Tiverton Junction.

The station area has now been developed for housing, but little else appears to have changed on 22 July 1990 (except for the brand of petrol sold!). *Peter Gray/DHM*

REAR COVER:
EXETER CENTRAL: The LSWR's route to Exeter was completed in 1860 and a terminus known as Queen Street was built in the Longbrook Valley, itself originally part of the moat of the nearby Norman Rougemont Castle. The original station was a small affair with an overall roof and was altered several times before complete re-building started in 1931. Official re-opening came on 1 July 1933 when the station was also given its present name. The eastern end is seen on 20 June 1964 as 'Merchant Navy' No 35025 *Brocklebank Line* approaches with the 3.00 pm Waterloo–Plymouth.

On 1 August 1990, Class '50' No 50044 *Exeter* is illustrated with the 15.15 Waterloo-Exeter St Davids. The 'A' signal box was closed in October 1984 when control of the station came under the Exeter power box. The up platform was shortened and the down through line removed as part of the associated work, whereas the up centre road had been taken out of use in 1969. The lines on either side of the signal box run to the goods yard, but do not see regular use following the cessation of cement traffic in January 1990. *Peter Gray/DHM*

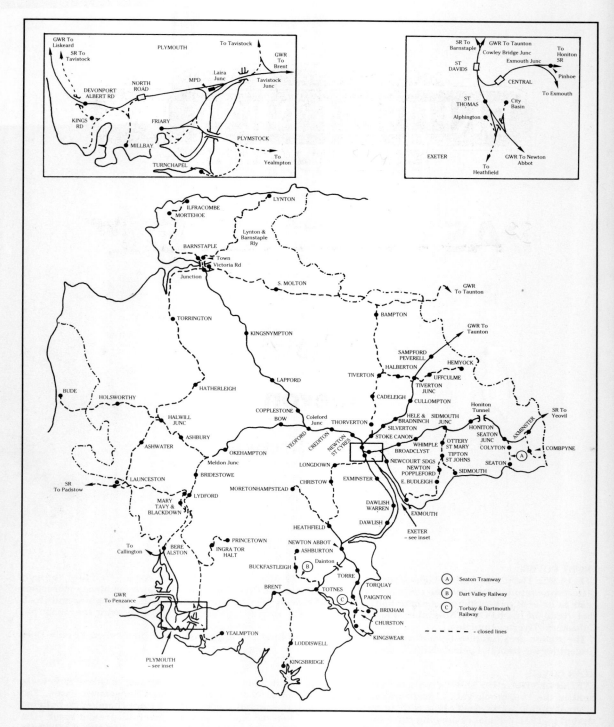

BRITISH RAILWAYS PAST & PRESENT No 8: DEVON – This book presents a detailed examination of the changing face of the railways in the county. The pictures have been chosen to provide a balanced view, including railways which are still in use or being developed, together with scenes where railways have been closed and either abandoned or redeveloped since the 'past' pictures were taken.

BRITISH RAILWAYS

PAST and PRESENT

No 8

Devon

David Mitchell

Past and Present

Past & Present Publishing Ltd

First published in May 1991
Reprinted July 1993
New edition with colour May 1994

British Library Cataloguing in Publication Data

A catalogue record for this book is available from the British Library

ISBN 1 85895 058 9

Past & Present Publishing Ltd
Unit 5
Home Farm Close
Church Street
Wadenhoe
Peterborough PE8 5TE
Tel/fax (0832) 720440

Printed and bound in Great Britain

CONTENTS

BIBLIOGRAPHY

If any reader wishes to investigate the railways of Devon in more detail, the following books are suggested, all of which have been referred to in caption research for this title.

General

A Regional History of the Railways of Great Britain, Vol I The West Country by David St John Thomas (David & Charles)

Atlas of the GWR by R. A. Cooke (Wild Swan)

Track Layout Diagrams of GWR, Vols 9, 12, 13, 14, 15 by R. A. Cooke

Ex-Southern lines

An Historical Survey of Southern Sheds by C. Hawkins & G. Reeve (OPC)

Atlantic Coast Express by S. Austin (Ian Allen)

The Sidmouth, Seaton & Lyme Regis Branches by C. Maggs & P. Paye (Oakwood)

Railways to Exmouth by C. Maggs (Oakwood)

The Withered Arm by T. W. E. Roche (Forge Books)

The Withered Arm by P. Semmens (Ian Allan)

The Barnstaple & Ilfracombe Railway by C. Maggs (Oakwood)

Lines to Torrington by J. Nicholas (OPC)

The Bude Branch by D. J. Wroe (Kingfisher)

Callington Railways by R. Cromblehome, B. Gibson, D. Stuckey & C. Whetmath (Forge Books)

The Turnchapel Branch by A. R. Kingdom (OPC)

Ex-GWR lines

The South Devon Railway by R. H. Gregory (Oakwood)

The Teign Valley Line by L. W. Pomroy (OPC)

The Brixham Branch by C. R. Potts (Oakwood)

The Exe Valley Railway by J. Owen (Kingfisher)

The Ashburton Branch by A. R. Kingdom (OPC)

The Kingsbridge Branch by K. Williams & D. Reynolds (OPC)

The Princetown branch by A. R. Kingdom (OPC)

The Tavistock, Launceston & Princetown Railways by G. H. Anthony (Oakwood)

The Yealmpton Branch by A. R. Kingdom (OPC)

An Historical Survey of GW Engine Sheds 1947 by E. Lyons (OPC)

TORRE was originally the terminus of a 5-mile branch opened by the South Devon Railway on 18 December 1848, and which started from a separate shed station in Newton Abbot. This location was known as Torquay at first, but was renamed when the line was extended to Paignton in 1859 (see page 103). On 10 May 1958, 0-4-2T No 1427 is departing with the 10.05 am Paignton–Moretonhampstead train, after taking water.

Today the station is an un-manned halt but still retains much of its character, particularly as the closed signal box is still standing. On 21 July 1990 Class '47' No 47848 passes with the 10.20 Paignton–York. *Peter Gray/DHM*

INTRODUCTION

Although it is the third largest county in England, the present-day population of Devonshire is only just over one million, thus reflecting its largely rural character with an economy traditionally based on agriculture. Despite this, railways proliferated during the railway building boom just as elsewhere in the country. Small towns were determined to join the ever-growing network, realising that they would soon lose their influence and trade if they did not.

The railway history of the area features the growth of two major companies, the Great Western and the London & South Western, each seeking to spread its influence, even if only to deny the progress of the other! This competition was further complicated by the GWR's choice of the 7-foot 'broad gauge'.

Through its antecedents the GWR was first on the scene and was able to develop a main line through the county with fast and frequent expresses, and fed by branch lines on either side. It also benefited from serving what were generally the wealthier areas, and it helped to enhance this prosperity. In contrast, the later arrival of the LSWR held back the economic development of the areas it served. In particular its network of lines west of Exeter, the so-called 'Withered Arm', did not warrant or indeed receive the level of service enjoyed to the south.

Despite this, only two ex-LSWR passenger lines (the narrow gauge Lynton & Barnstaple, and the Turnchapel branch) had closed prior to the publication of the Beeching report in 1963, whereas half of Devon's former GWR branches had passed into oblivion by then. Subsequently, though, the former LSWR routes were to be decimated, as detailed in the following pages.

As an enthusiast it is easy to over-sentimentalise the closure of any railway, and it has to be admitted that some routes had probably outlasted their value. Although not a typical example, it is arguable that the ND&CJLR (Torrington to Halwill) line was an anachronism when it opened in 1925, and its survival as a passenger line for 40 years must rate as something of a miracle, or a reflection upon a remote management lacking in financial acumen. Possibly if earlier attempts had been made at cost-cutting and modernisation, the wholesale closures of the 1950s and 1960s might have been partly avoided.

When it came, the dieselisation of the South West was a quick process as the area was earmarked by BR's Western Region authorities for the early eradication of steam. This led to the short-lived diesel-hydraulic era, now also a part of history, but a fascinating period in itself, and I am pleased to be able to include a number of rare views in these pages.

Today it is gratifying to report that the former GWR main line is thriving with frequent and well-patronised services to London, the Midlands and the North. As elsewhere, the coming of the HST captured the public's imagination and currently the fastest train of the day allows a journey from Exeter to London in only 2 hours 4 minutes.

No passenger routes have closed since the Kingswear line was sold in 1972, whilst stations have reopened – the success of Tiverton Parkway is a hopeful indication for the future. At the time of writing there is a suggestion that the Bere Alston to Tavistock line could be reopened as part of Plymouth's plans to overcome road congestion.

After years as a 'Cinderella' route, the ex-LSWR main line has undergone something of a revival, and Exeter Central is now the western outpost of Network Southeast. Unfortunately the once-hoped-for extension of the third rail does not now look likely, and the increasingly unreliable Class '50s' are now due to be replaced by Class '159' 'Sprinters' in 1992.

Freight tonnage has never been particularly high in this area and the viability of present Railfreight operations is largely dependent on clay traffic, some of which originates in Devon but the majority of which passes through *en route* from the main producing areas in Cornwall. There is, however, an interesting variety of traffic, some of which is recorded in this volume, but the current demise of Speedlink operations is a cause for concern.

It is to be hoped that the growing environmental lobby will encourage the government to develop a more enlightened view on railway matters and that any future similar book will be able to report on an expanding rather than a contracting system.

All the 'present' photographs were taken during 1990 especially for this title. An attempt was made to stand in the same spot as the earlier photographers, but this has not always proved possible. In particular, Devon's mild climate has led to many scenes becoming totally overgrown, and rather than either pursue a policy of deforestation or include a series of botanical studies, some different viewpoints have been selected where considered appropriate.

I am most grateful to those photographers who have so willingly provided archive material, and who are credited individually throughout this book. My sincere thanks are also offered to John Medley for his help with this project, to Ron Lumber and Eric Youldon for their assistance with the captions, and to those individuals who kindly allowed me access to their private property to enable some of the modern pictures to be taken.

David Mitchell
Exeter

The Bristol & Exeter and associated lines

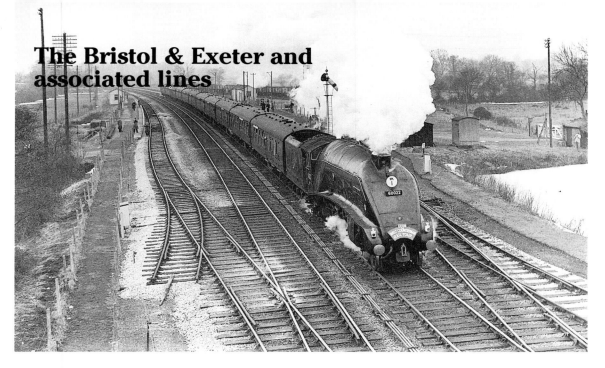

SAMPFORD PEVERELL HALT/TIVERTON PARKWAY: The broad gauge reached Devon when the Bristol & Exeter Railway was opened through to its destination on 1 May 1844. The previous limit of operations was a temporary station at Beambridge, just west of Wellington, and the extension from there included the 1,088-yard long Whiteball tunnel which also marked the Somerset/Devon boundary. Sampford Peverell Halt was situated some 4 miles from the border, serving a nearby village. The track here was quadrupled in 1932, with platform loops, and the layout is shown clearly as 'A4' 'Pacific' No 60022 *Mallard* passes with the LCGB's 'The West Countryman Rail Tour' on 24 February 1963. The Gresley 4-6-2 had earlier worked from Waterloo to Exeter before handing over its train to two '45XX' tanks for a journey along the Exe Valley and Tiverton lines to Tiverton Junction. *Peter Gray*

The halt was closed from 5 October 1964 and there was little to indicate that it had ever existed by 28 August 1982 when Class '47' No 47482 passed with a Paignton to Nottingham train. Happily, though, that is not the end of the story, as due to its strategic position adjacent to both the M5 motorway and North Devon Link Road, the site was selected as a suitable location for a new station, replacing the rather less convenient Tiverton Junction. *DHM*

TIVERTON PARKWAY was opened on 12 May 1986 by the Rt Hon David Mitchell MP, Minister of State for Transport, with the £730,000 funding provided by InterCity, Devon County Council and Mid Devon District Council. Initially 12 trains in each direction were provided each day, but such has been its success that currently 36 trains call each weekday. Passing this stylish station on 14 July 1990 is an HST forming the 9.40 Newquay–Glasgow. The power cars are 43178 and 43136. *DHM*

TIVERTON JUNCTION (1): This was one of the original B&E stations opened in 1844 as Tiverton Road. It was subsequently rebuilt and renamed in 1848 when the Tiverton branch opened. Substantial rebuilding took place in 1932 resulting in the layout visible in the photograph of 0-4-2T No 1462 as it adds four milk tanks to the rear of an up passenger train on 24 February 1962. The Tiverton branch curved away to the left whilst the Hemyock branch coach can be seen in the distance behind the loco's chimney, and a travelling gas wagon can be glimpsed in the yard.

The station lost much of its raison d'être following closure of these branches, but it remained the only intermediate station between Taunton and Exeter until closure on 9 May 1986. The signal box had closed on 3 March 1986 and was demolished on 30 March 1990. The platform loops have been retained, however, and the location is now known as Tiverton Loop. Passing on 16 July 1990 is Class '47' No 47318 with the 10.44 Fawley–Tavistock Junction Esso tanks. *Terry Nicholls/DHM*

TIVERTON JUNCTION (2): The second branch to leave this station was the Culm Valley line to Hemyock, and this ran from the outer face of the down platform. The scene on 19 February 1973 is one of activity with Class '52' No D1010 *Western Campaigner* standing in the up platform with 7C52, the 10.10 St Blazey – Severn Tunnel Junction freight, waiting to be overtaken, whilst Class '25' No 7677 (later 25327) sets out with two empty milk tanks for its journey down the branch. The 'Western' has been preserved by Foster Yeoman and is presently on the West Somerset Railway under the guise of D1035 *Western Yeoman*.

It is not possible to exactly reproduce the angle today as the footbridge was truncated after closure of the station, when Redland Tiles started using the former car park as a loading area for their products. Unfortunately this traffic was suspended at the end of March 1990, but the siding still contains empty wagons on 2 June as Class '47' No 47821 *Royal Worcester* leads DVT No 82129 on the 7.31 Wolverhampton–Penzance. *Both DHM*

HEMYOCK was the terminus of the branch and is illustrated on 7 September 1963 as No 1421 arrives with ex-LNER coaches Nos W87270E and W87245E on the 5.10 pm from Tiverton Junction, the very last passenger train. These short coaches had been introduced only the previous year to replace two ex-Barry Railway gas-lit vehicles. Behind the photographer was the United Dairies creamery, milk from which provided the bulk of the line's income and ensured its survival until October 1975. At that time the M5 was under construction near Tiverton Junction and originally provision was made for the motorway to bridge the branch. However, the closure of the creamery led to the infilling of this section. St Ivel Foods now occupy the creamery premises and have also taken over the station site, partly as a car park. *R. A. Lumber/DHM*

HALBERTON HALT was the only intermediate station on the Tiverton branch, a broad gauge line opened by the B&E on 12 June 1848 and 'narrowed' in 1884. It was originally intended that the route would be double track and consequently the overbridges had a wide span. This halt was built beneath the bridge carrying the road from the village of Halberton, using the available space for the platform, and was opened on 5 December 1927. In this evocative photograph taken on a freezing 2 February 1963, 0-4-2T No 1421 and its auto-coach head for Tiverton Junction through the wintry waste.

The passenger service ended on 3 October 1964, with goods traffic ceasing on 5 June 1967. Today the formation has been levelled with the adjoining fields, as seen in July 1990. *Peter Gray/DHM*

CULLOMPTON is an important market town which merited having a station on the opening of the B&E to Exeter. It was also one of those locations selected for quadrupling of the track to ease congestion, particularly at summer weekends, with the work completed by the end of 1931. Unfortunately the volume of through traffic meant that it did not enjoy a particularly intensive service, as with other stations between Taunton and Exeter. However, on 19 April 1962 large 'Prairie' tank No 4165 is pictured departing with a down stopper.

The station closed from 5 October 1964, with the loops taken out of use in 1969. The decaying goods shed is still standing as 'Cromptons' Nos 33114 and 33110 rumble by with 6V96, the 9.38 Tonbridge–Meldon on 20 August 1990. *R. A. Lumber/DHM*

HELE & BRADNINCH was another of the original B&E stations of 1844, when it was named simply Hele, its actual location; the additional name refers to a separate but larger village nearby. On 5 August 1957, Collett 4-6-0 No 6021 *King Richard II* thunders through on the 6.25 am Penzance–Paddington. The station closed in October 1964 but the signal box, which is just visible in the left foreground, survived until 9 December 1985 when it was closed as part of the Exeter MAS scheme. It latterly controlled the adjacent level crossing and goods loops.

Today both the main station building and goods shed still stand, the latter used by a motor trader. On 5 August 1990 Class '37' No 37718 grinds past with an Exeter City Basin–Cardiff Tidal Sidings scrap metal train. This traffic was previously conveyed in Speedlink workings, but from June 1990 this weekly Metals sub-sector block train was introduced. *Peter Gray/DHM*

SILVERTON (1): Seemingly in the tradition of many of Devon's country stations, the village of Silverton is $1^1/2$ miles distant via the road from which these photos were taken. On 9 December 1961, the basic down platform is in view as small 'Prairie' No 5560 returns from the goods yard to rejoin its train in the up refuge siding. This Exeter Riverside to Tiverton Junction pick-up goods will pursue a leisurely journey including stops at Stoke Canon and Hele & Bradninch *en route*.

Closure came on 3 October 1964 and there is no evidence of the station's existence on 14 July 1990 as Brush Class '47' No 47820 powers by with the 10.20 Paignton–York. *Peter Gray/DHM*

SILVERTON (2): The station possessed staggered platforms and in this second 9 December 1961 view the up side can be seen along with GWR 4-6-0 No 5055 *Earl of Eldon* on the 9.40 Cardiff–Plymouth. This working was a substitution for an InterCity DMU which was unavailable due to heating problems. Just visible behind the 'Castle's' exhaust is the original platform-mounted signal box, closed in 1928 when a new box was opened. The latter can be observed on the right, next to the small goods yard from where a trace of steam comes from 2-6-2T No 5560. A line trailed away from here to serve a paper mill. Today the scene is typically overgrown as HST power cars Nos 43032 and 43188 speed the 7.00 Manchester–Newquay by. *Peter Gray/DHM*

STOKE CANON is pictured on 3 June 1961 as D600 *Active* passes with a Paddington train. The original station was ¼ mile further north with staggered platforms on either side of a level crossing, but a new station opened on 1 July 1894 at the junction with the Exe Valley branch. A further transformation took place when the line was quadrupled and the rebuilt station included an island platform on the up road with the far side serving the branch trains. The 'Warship' was one of the original five diesel-hydraulics built by the North British Loco Co in 1957/8. This was against the wishes of WR authorities who wanted lightweight locos, but they eventually had their way when a further order was cancelled in favour of the Class '43'. Passenger services had ceased at Stoke Canon exactly a year before but the platform loops survived for goods trains for a few more years.

Today the main building is in commercial use and on 22 July 1990 Class '47' No 47439 passes, also with a Paddington service. *R. A. Lumber/DHM*

CADELEIGH, on the Exe Valley line, had a passing loop and was originally known as Cadeleigh & Bickleigh, with renaming effective from 1 May 1906. It was situated adjacent to the main Exeter to Tiverton road, and was thus particularly susceptible to road competition, the main reason for closure of the whole line to passengers on 7 October 1963. Pictured on 16 March 1963, 0-6-0PT No 6400 leaves on the 15.25 service from Exeter. The site is now used as a road depot by Devon County Council and the buildings are remarkably intact, as recorded on 8 July 1990. *Peter Gray/DHM*

THORVERTON was the first crossing place on the Exe Valley line. It opened with the branch on 1 May 1885, and the layout is shown clearly in this view at 2.30 pm on 12 March 1960 as a Class '14XX' tank with auto-coach stands with an Exeter train whilst 2-6-2T No 5524 leaves for Tiverton. The cattle loading dock adjoins the goods shed, with a 5-ton crane nearby. Just ahead of the 'Prairie' tank, a line curves away to the right to serve a mill, also just visible. This siding was added in 1898 and the branch from here to the main line survived until 30 November 1966 for grain traffic.

The station building is now a dwelling with the accommodation extended by the use of stonework from the demolished goods shed. Another house has been erected on the site of the goods yard. *Peter Gray/DHM*

BAMPTON: The Exe Valley line actually comprised two railways, the Tiverton & North Devon being the first to open its route to Dulverton on 1 August 1884, almost a year before the actual Exe Valley commenced operations south of Tiverton. Whilst the latter came under GWR ownership before opening, the former was nominally independent for ten years, although it was always worked by the GWR. The town of Bampton is most famous for its annual Pony Fair, where each autumn Exmoor ponies are sold, and for many years this provided traffic for the railway. On 16 March 1963, 0-4-2T No 1450 is pictured awaiting departure with the 3.20 pm to Exeter.

After closure this area was partly filled in and levelled for a road improvement, with a car park behind. The reference points to link these views are the buildings behind the station, which are just discernible through the trees today. *Peter Gray/DHM*

The Southern in East Devon

AXMINSTER: The LSWR route to Devon enters the county by following the Axe Valley, the first station being here. On a very wet 28 June 1953, 'T9' 4-4-0 No 30711 is standing in the down platform with an RCTS 25th Anniversary Special. Behind it is the small goods yard containing a string of cattle wagons, whilst in the background is the carpet factory for which the town is famous. Out of view on the right is the bay platform for the Lyme Regis branch which started on the north side of the main line but then crossed it by means to a flyover before heading south.

Axminster is now the railhead for a large area of East Devon and West Dorset but the station has only a single track through it. On 22 July 1990, Class '50' No 50048 *Dauntless* arrives on the 14.45 Plymouth–Waterloo. To the left of this scene the main station building is still standing, but apparently is in a poor condition; as this book goes to press there are plans for its demolition. *Peter Gray/DHM*

COMBPYNE was the only intermediate station on the Axminster & Lyme Regis Light Railway, which opened on 24 August 1903. It possessed a crossing loop until 1930 when it was removed as an economy measure, although a siding survived for goods traffic until this facility was withdrawn in February 1964. The low axle limit and sharp curvature of the track caused problems in finding suitable locos for the line, and these were not solved until an ageing Adams 4-4-2T was successfully tested in 1913. Eventually three of the class were based at Exmouth Junction to work the line and were not ousted until 1961 when '2MT' 2-6-2Ts were introduced. No 30583 is seen departing with the 5.10 pm from Lyme Regis on 11 May 1957. This particular engine was purchased by the Bluebell Railway on 9 July 1961 where it is now restored as LSWR No 488. A camping coach can just be seen in the siding.

The branch was dieselised from November 1963 and closed from 29 November 1965. Today the station building is a private house, and a lawn covers the site of the trackbed and 250-ft island platform. *Peter Gray/DHM*

SEATON JUNCTION (1): The LSWR line from Yeovil Junction to Exeter was opened on 18 July 1860, and Colyton for Seaton was one of the original stations. With the opening of the Seaton branch on 16 March 1868 it was renamed Colyton Junction, with yet another change to Seaton Junction the following year to avoid confusion with Colyton itself. Considerable reconstruction took place in 1927/8 when through lines were provided, and this layout is shown on 30 July 1960 as Class 'N15' 'King Arthur' 4-6-0 No 30451 *Sir Lamorak* calls with a down stopper at 3.25 pm. Prominent are the tall up starter signals, which were necessary as the view through the station was obscured by a curve and two footbridges. A duplicate lower set of signal arms are mounted for drivers stopped in the station.

Thirty years on (12 August 1990) the scene is one of dereliction as Class '50' No 50048 *Dauntless* speeds through with the 13.00 Waterloo–Exeter. The station buildings are now in commercial use. *R. A. Lumber/DHM*

SEATON JUNCTION (2): The west end of the station on 11 June 1962, as 'S15' 4-6-0 No 30823 heads for Vauxhall after marshalling its milk train from the Express Dairies depot. The signal box was positioned on the end of the down platform just to the left of this photograph, whilst the lines trailing to the left led to the Seaton branch platform which curved away quite sharply. The station closed with the branch on 7 March 1966.

When the main line was singled the down through road was retained, but in October 1972 the track was slewed to the site of the former up through line, and it is over this formation that No 50001 *Dreadnought* travels on 22 July 1990 with the 14.28 Exeter–Waterloo. *Peter Gray/DHM*

SEATON JUNCTION (3): The Seaton branch platform is pictured on Saturday 30 July 1960 as 'M7' 0-4-4T No 30048 arrives with a through Seaton to Waterloo working. This area has now merged with the adjoining field and the house on the horizon is the easiest way to link the past and present views. Part of the platform does, however, survive to the left of this present-day scene. *R. A. Lumber/DHM*

A view from the branch platform on 13 February 1965 shows GWR 0-4-2T No 1450 waiting to leave with a Seaton train. *Geoff Lendon*

COLYTON station on 27 February 1965, as GWR 0-4-2T No 1442 approaches, propelling its auto-trailer from Seaton. The branch had been dieselised from 4 November 1963, but a shortage of DMUs through failures led to the temporary use of this engine and sister No 1450. The station once boasted two sidings, but these had been removed in May 1964.

After closure of the branch, a tramway company previously based in Eastbourne obtained an option on 3 miles of the trackbed with a view to transferring their operations. Eventually in August 1970 services commenced over the 2 ft 9 in gauge track from Seaton to Colyford, with the northern extension to Colyton opening in 1979. On 22 July 1990 one of the tramcars departs for Seaton. *Peter Gray/DHM*

SEATON: Like most of Devon's branch lines, the Seaton & Beer Railway started life as an independent company, but was sold to the LSWR in 1888. That company had worked the line from its opening and a variety of locomotive types was employed over the years, culminating in the regular use of 'M7' 0-4-4Ts. Later, along with the rest of the Southern Region west of Salisbury, the branch was transferred to the Western in 1963, and GWR '64XX' 0-6-0PTs were introduced in May of that year. On 29 June 1963 No 6400 itself is portrayed on a wet day after its tanks have been replenished. The tramway does not run to the original station in Seaton and an electronics factory has now been built on the site. *Peter Gray/DHM*

HONITON BANK stretches from just east of Seaton Junction to a summit inside the west end of the 1,353-yard Honiton Tunnel. Seven miles long, with much of it at a gradient of 1 in 80, the bank presented a challenge to the crews on down trains, but not for the men on the footplate of 'West Country' 4-6-2 No 34033 *Chard* as they descend the bank on 30 August 1964 with the 15.25 Exeter Central–Yeovil Junction. The manicured cutting sides present a considerable contrast with the 12 August 1990 view of Class '50' No 50043 *Eagle* on the 14.45 Plymouth–Waterloo. *R. A. Lumber/DHM*

SIDMOUTH JUNCTION (1): Feniton station was opened on 18 July 1860 but then underwent a series of name changes before becoming Sidmouth Junction when the Sidmouth branch opened. It is under that identity that the east end of the site is shown on 3 August 1964 in this superb action photograph as two rebuilt Bulleid 'Pacifics' meet. 'Merchant Navy' No 35020 *Bibby Line* is on the 3.00 pm Waterloo–Plymouth, whilst 'West Country' No 34014 *Budleigh Salterton* approaches with the 5.45 pm Exeter Central–Waterloo. On the left is the goods yard with the Sidmouth line trailing away to the south.

On 10 June 1990, a similar viewpoint captures Class '50' No 50016 *Barham* on the 11.05 Paignton–Waterloo. This locomotive suffered a power unit failure only nine days later and has now been withdrawn. *Peter Gray/DHM*

SIDMOUTH JUNCTION (2): On the station's last day (4 March 1967), the view from the short down platform shows a three-car DMU departing with the 5.54 pm Exeter Central-Salisbury. On the left is the solitary up siding and tall LSWR signal box, whilst the goods yard and Sidmouth bay are on the right.

Subsequent housing development adjacent to the railway brought about its re-opening under its original name on 3 May 1971, mainly to cater for commuter traffic into Exeter. The former down platform was reinstated, and on 28 May 1990 No 50002 *Superb* arrives with a Waterloo to Exeter St Davids service. *R. A. Lumber/DHM*

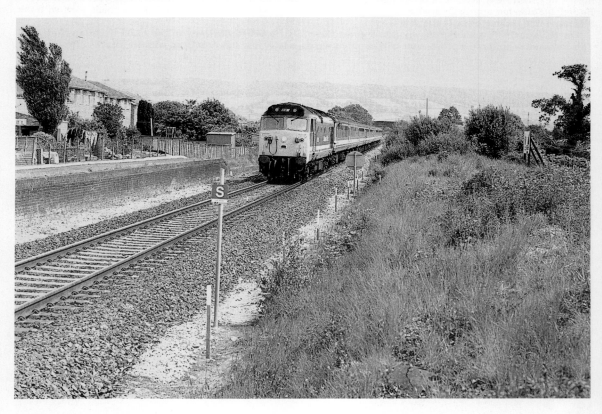

OTTERY ST MARY was the first station on the Sidmouth Railway which opened on 6 July 1874 and remained nominally independent until 1922, although worked from the outset by the LSWR. This location possessed a passing loop which can be seen as NBL Class '22' No D6312 pauses with the Waterloo–Exmouth through train on Saturday 17 July 1965. Another portion of this train had preceded it to Sidmouth behind 'Hymek' Class '35' No D7070. This was the last year that such a through service ran over these lines. The signal box had opened on 20 November 1955, replacing the original box which stood on the opposite side of the track. The site is now occupied by Devon County Council, with the station building occupied as a youth club in this 1 April 1990 view. *R. A. Lumber/DHM*

TIPTON ST JOHNS was only originally a passing station on the Sidmouth line, but on 14 May 1897 it also became junction for the Budleigh Salterton Railway. At its peak, this was a very busy location with over 50 trains a day calling. On 25 February 1967 the 15.53 Sidmouth–Sidmouth Junction is arriving, having just descended the 1 in 45 incline visible behind the train. Also in view is the signal box which controlled the crossing gates. The station is now a dwelling, and the present owner has restored the platform canopy, as depicted on 28 May 1990. *R. A. Lumber/DHM*

SIDMOUTH on 28 February 1965 as 0-6-0PT No 4666 leaves with the LCGB 'East Devon Railtour', with the large goods shed visible behind the first coach. A long-standing health resort, Sidmouth has always prided itself on being a select holiday town and many inhabitants viewed the coming of the railway as a mixed blessing. It is suggested that the location of the station, some ³/₄ mile inland, was done deliberately to discourage daytrippers. Notwithstanding this, there is little doubt that the town profited from its rail service until closure from 6 March 1967.

The station site has now been developed as a small industrial estate, and it is not possible to produce an exact 'present' photo. However, the May 1990 view shows the former goods shed, together with a newer building erected where the platform once was. *R. A. Lumber/DHM*

NEWTON POPPLEFORD was opened on 1 June 1899 and possessed a single platform with a goods siding parallel to it. Goods services ceased from 27 January 1964 and the siding was lifted the following year. On the last day of passenger services, 4 March 1967, a DMU calls with an Exmouth to Sidmouth train which will have to reverse at Tipton St Johns.

The site is now privately owned, but is yet to see any development. The platform survived intact for many years, but has now been excavated, as discovered on 1 April 1990. *R. A. Lumber/DHM*

EAST BUDLEIGH station was actually within the boundaries of the village of Otterton, but it is thought that it was so-named to avoid confusion with Otterham on the North Cornwall line. It was located on the Budleigh Salterton Railway, which opened on 14 May 1897 and was extended to Exmouth on 1 June 1903. The 'past' view shows a DMU forming the 15.40 Exmouth–Sidmouth Junction on 18 June 1966.

The station has now been converted into a private house, but this May 1990 view from the road bridge is obscured by trees that have grown in the trackbed. Just visible through these, however, is a white line marking the platform edge, whilst fencing on the left delineates the boundary with the neighbouring field. *R. A. Lumber/DHM*

EXMOUTH (1): The station is depicted on 6 September 1963 as Standard Class '4' 2-6-4T No 80037 arrives with the 5.49 pm from Exeter Central, three days before dieselisation of the branch services. This line opened on 1 May 1861, and has always carried substantial volumes of passengers, particularly commuters who are able to travel easily into the centre of Exeter. The relatively fast journey, coupled with well-sited stations, has sustained business in the face of road competition. Despite this, closure was proposed in the Beeching report, and although it was reprieved, economies were made and the line singled throughout, other than for a passing loop at Topsham. *R. A. Lumber/DHM*

EXMOUTH JUNCTION MPD was opened in 1887 on a green field site on the outskirts of Exeter, replacing a small depot at Queen Street (Central) station. It was substantially rebuilt during 1923-9, creating the 13-road building pictured here, which also shows an interesting variety of SR and BR steam classes, including no fewer than eight Bulleid 'Pacifics'. Exmouth Junction was the SR's main shed in the South West with an allocation of over 100 locos. The depot was closed to steam in 1965, with total closure in March 1967 and demolition in 1970. The site lay derelict until 1979 when a supermarket was built. *Terry Nicholls/DHM*

In this further view, taken on 6 March 1965, Ivatt 2-6-2T No 41206, GWR '57XX' 0-6-0PT No 4694 and BR 2-6-2T No 82042 stand alongside the depot. *Geoff Lendon*

NEWCOURT SIDINGS on the Exmouth branch were laid by United States troops and brought into use on 23 January 1944. The sidings, which were controlled by their own signal box until 1973, were latterly used by the Ministry of Defence to serve a Naval stores depot. On 11 August 1978 Class '25' 'Rat' No 25225 shunts its thrice-weekly trip working from Exeter Riverside yard.

By the turn of the decade, the traffic had become quite irregular, and despite a revival of activity during the Falklands War in 1982, closure occurred soon afterwards. The site in June 1990 provides a scene of dereliction, although both the loading gauge and shed still stand. *Both DHM*

EXETER CENTRAL: The western approach on 18 May 1965 as Ivatt '2MT' 2-6-2T No 41249 shunts empty stock during the last week of regular steam activity in the area. It was at this station that expresses were split for the Plymouth/North Cornwall and North Devon lines and engines for these trains would stand here whilst waiting to back down on to their portion. On the right is the start of the 1 in 37 descent to Exeter St Davids which opened on 1 February 1862. Just out of sight is the 184-yard St Davids Tunnel.

The sidings were removed in February 1970 and the site is now a car park. No 50001 *Dreadnought* storms past on 10 June 1990 with the 17.22 Exeter–Waterloo. Use of the down line by up trains is now possible following re-signalling. *R. A. Lumber/DHM*

50

EXETER ST DAVIDS (1): The station dates from 1844 when the B&E reached the city. Two years later the South Devon was opened and, with the subsequent opening of the Exeter & Crediton in 1851 and the arrival of the LSWR in 1862, it became a major railway crossroads and the most important station in Devon. The LSWR had reached agreement for its trains to run through the station over the B&E metals but as a result it had to stop all trains there. Their different approaches to the location also meant that up Paddington and Waterloo workings travelled in opposite directions. The original station was inadequate for the extra traffic and was rebuilt during 1862-4, whilst the present facilities date from a further reconstruction in 1911-4 when only the frontage was retained.

The east end is shown on 20 August 1963 as 'W' Class 2-6-4T No 31915 approaches with a transfer freight from Riverside Yard to Exmouth Junction. On the left, sister engine No 31924 waits to provide banking assistance to Central station. The modern view on 4 August 1990 shows Class '50' No 50023 *Howe* entering with the empty stock of the 16.22 departure to Waterloo. *R. A. Lumber/DHM*

51

EXETER ST DAVIDS (2): On 3 May 1964 heavy freight 2-8-0 No 2887 stands in the yard with the stock for 'The Cornubian' railtour which it will work as far as Plymouth, where 'West Country' No 34002 *Salisbury* will take over for the final steam run over the Cornish main line to Penzance. On the left is the coal stage for the engine shed, with its ramp approach, the depot being hidden by the train.

The shed had closed in 1963 and eventually the roof was removed, although the side walls remain, and more recently a diesel maintenance shed and fuelling point have been erected and can be noted in the 10 June 1990 scene. Among the power on display are Nos 50015 *Valiant*, 47520 and 08849. The new power box is just to the left of this scene. *R. A. Lumber/DHM*

EXETER ST THOMAS opened on 30 May 1846 when the South Devon Railway commenced operations to Teignmouth using hired GWR engines, the atmospheric system not being ready until the following year. The station was built on a 62-arch brick and stone viaduct and had a typical Brunel timber overall roof. By 10 July 1970 the roof had decayed badly and work on its demolition had started as Class '52' No D1037 *Western Empress* passed with the 12.25 Penzance–Paddington.

Today the station is an unmanned halt which is pictured on 3 June 1990 as Class '37s' Nos 37671 *Tre Pol & Pen* and 37414 rumble through with 6S55, the 11.45 Burngullow–Irvine. The train comprises 11 tanks of china clay slurry, the maximum allowed over the South Devon banks, and another four will be added to the consist in Riverside Yard. This service started in 1989 and the round trip of 1,100 miles is BR's longest block freight working, with the Laira '37s' in charge throughout. *John Medley/DHM*

EXETER CITY BASIN: A broad gauge branch line, less than half a mile in length, was opened in June 1867 to link the SDR with Exeter's ancient ship canal. The down line from St Davids was altered to mixed gauge in October 1876 and from then until the abolition of the broad gauge in 1892, the daily goods could comprise wagons of both gauges. On 1 October 1958, GWR 0-6-0PT No 9629 engages in shunting activity in the basin area. The sidings were abandoned in 1968 but a loop survives, the end of which is just visible in the modern view of 20 May 1990.

Running from this loop were tracks serving the Gas Works, operated at one time by two Peckett 0-4-0STs. No 2031 of 1942 is now preserved on the Dart Valley, but is shown at its previous home on 1 February 1969. *R. A. Lumber/DHM/John Medley*

54

Routes to North Devon

COWLEY BRIDGE JUNCTION: The development of a route to North Devon was hindered by the conflicting interests of the GWR and LSWR, but eventually the Exeter & Crediton Railway was opened on 12 May 1851 as a double track broad gauge route, leased to the B&E and leaving the latter's line at this junction. Subsequently the line's lease was transferred to the LSWR from 1862 and mixed gauge introduced. However, the rival GWR continued to run a daily goods train to Crediton until 1903. In the 'past' picture, two 'Battle of Britain' 'Pacifics' meet on 25 November 1961 as No 34070 *Manston* heads towards Exeter with the up 'Atlantic Coast Express', passing No 34056 *Croydon* (with coal spray in use) on the 11.47 am Exeter Central to Plymouth stopper.

Following the rebuilding of three nearby bridges, the former SR route was singled across them and over the junction on 28 November 1965, while the signal box closed on 30 March 1985 as part of the Exeter MAS scheme. On 16 July 1990, Class '47' No 47291 *The Port of Felixstowe* passes with the 04.50 MO Gloucester–Tavistock Junction Speedlink working. *Peter Gray/DHM*

NEWTON ST CYRES: The Exeter & Crediton followed the Yeo Valley, with the only intermediate station being here. The location is illustrated on 23 August 1963 as 'N' 2-6-0 No 31836 passes with a goods for Exeter. Until 17 August 1930 the station boasted a signal box which stood on a site approximately level with the locomotive, but from that date the frame was removed to the booking office. The small goods yard closed on 12 September 1960 and the track was removed in December 1962; the line to Crediton was singled in December 1984.

On 2 July 1990, 'Cromptons' Nos 33103 and 33201 pass the station with 6V93, the 13.40 Hoo Junction–Meldon Quarry, comprising 28 empty 'Seacow' and 'Sealion' wagons. These locos are currently in a pool of 11 Southern Region Class '33s' dedicated to departmental traffic from Meldon. *Peter Gray/DHM*

CREDITON is recorded on 26 June 1982 as Class '31' No 31286 approaches the station with the 10.05 Barnstaple–Exeter. The signalman can be glimpsed standing in front of his box as he waits to receive the single-line token. Under modern signalling, on 13 June 1990, DCWA Class '50' No 50008 *Thunderer* stands at Crediton waiting to cross the 11.20 Meldon–Tonbridge. The loco is working light engine to Meldon Quarry from where it will head the 13.35 departure to Bristol East Depot. *Both DHM*

Although Crediton's semaphore signals have now gone, fortunately the LSWR signal box survives and acts as a 'fringe' box to the Exeter panel. *DHM*

YEOFORD (1): The North Devon Railway commenced operations on 1 August 1854 from Crediton to Barnstaple as a broad gauge line. The LSWR acquired the lease on 1 January 1863 and the route was converted to mixed gauge. Originally there was single track, but Crediton to Coleford Junction was doubled in the 1870s. Yeoford is one mile south of the latter location and thus despite only serving a small village, it became an important railway centre with the re-marshalling of goods trains to and from the Plymouth and North Devon lines. The yard was also used as holding sidings with a pool of cattle wagons for use on the 'Withered Arm' routes.

On 9 March 1968, a two-car DMU departs with an Exeter-Barnstaple service, while in a much rationalised scene on 5 May 1990, Derby 'Lightweight' Class '108' set No P956 passes with the 14.41 Barnstaple–Exeter. *R. A. Lumber/DHM*

In an earlier view on 28 June 1951, GWR 2-6-0 No 6319 is pictured with a Plymouth train. *Tom Reardon*

YEOFORD (2): A 24 September 1967 view from the other side of the road bridge that straddles this location shows Class '22' diesel-hydraulic No D6310 with four milk tanks from Lapford. A tall signal box which allowed the signalman a clear view over the bridge stood just to the left, but this was closed on 18 August 1968 when all of the track was taken out of use apart from the two running lines. A similar viewpoint on 5 May 1990 shows Departmental Class '50' No 50020 *Revenge* returning from Meldon Quarry with Pathfinder Tours' 'Taw & Tor Tourer'. *R. A. Lumber/DHM*

CHURSTON station, on the Kingswear branch, was recorded at 10.23 am on 11 March 1960 just after the 10.15 am mixed train off the Brixham branch had arrived in the charge of '14XX' 0-4-2T No 1470. Other than fish trains that ran as required, by this time no exclusively freight service operated over the branch, and the goods traffic, mainly household coal, was included in the 7.35 am from Churston and this return working.

Since the first edition of 'British Railways Past and Present' No 8 was prepared, a new workshop has been erected by the Paignton & Dartmouth Steam Railway, and this rather dominates the present-day scene. This more modern image is completed on 20 June 1992 as the line's Class '25', No D7535, departs with a Kingswear to Paignton train during a Diesel Gala. *Peter W. Gray/David Mitchell*

CORNWALL LOOP JUNCTION: When the Cornwall Railway opened from Truro to Plymouth Millbay on 4 May 1859, it connected with the South Devon at Cornwall Junction, about half a mile north of the latter station. The LSWR opened a loop from Plymouth North Road to Cornwall Loop Junction in May 1876 for its trains to Devonport, enabling them to bypass Millbay. Subsequently the GWR also used this loop, and it became part of its main line to Cornwall. On 2 May 1959 an RCTS centenary railtour comprising No 6420 and auto-coaches is illustrated as it crosses Stonehouse Pool Viaduct on its way from Saltash to Millbay. Cornwall Loop Viaduct is on the right of the picture, while the original SDR route is out of sight below the photographer.

The curve from Cornwall Loop Junction to Cornwall Junction closed on 16 January 1964. The foreground has since been built up, and recently a dog-walking footpath and community green has been created. On 31 December 1993 the 10.35 Paddington-Penzance HST crosses Cornwall Loop Viaduct. Part of Stonehouse Pool Viaduct survives, and one of its girders (painted red) can be seen. *Peter W. Gray/David Mitchell*

The 'Withered Arm'

BOW was the first station on the Devon & Cornwall Railway opening as Nymet Tracey on 1 November 1865 when services commenced on the initial section to North Tawton. Progress on extending this line was slow, but Okehampton Road (later Belstone Corner, and later still Sampford Courtenay!) was reached in 1867, and Okehampton itself was served from 3 October 1871. Eventually this route was to become part of the LSWR's main line to Plymouth, but after closure between Okehampton and Bere Alston in 1968, Bow was served by a DMU shuttle which operated between Exeter and Okehampton. Pictured on 1 May 1969, Pressed Steel Class '121' single unit No W55034 pauses with the 15.35 from Exeter St Davids.

The line was singled on 17 October 1971 and regular passenger services withdrawn on 5 June 1972. Freight traffic continued to Okehampton for a while but now the route survives only for stone trains from Meldon Quarry. The station building is privately owned, but the platforms are becoming overgrown, as shown on 13 June 1990 as Class '33s' Nos 33008 *Eastleigh* and 33117 thunder past with 7V80, the 04.08 from Woking. Although in a poor condition, the shelter still stands on the former up platform. *R. A. Lumber/DHM*

OKEHAMPTON is a market town bordering the Dartmoor National Park. With the junction of the Plymouth and North Cornwall lines being less than 3 miles to the west it also became a railway centre. It was from here that a motorail service to Surbiton ran from 1960-4, enabling holidaymakers to beat the traffic jams prevalent at such places as the notorious Exeter bypass. The cars were loaded in the sidings to the left of Standard 2-6-4T No 80041, which is climbing away from the station with the 7.40 pm to Bude on 4 August 1964, although on this occasion the sidings contain a ballast train from Meldon Quarry.

Dating from 1897, the quarry is a wholly owned subsidiary of BR and presently produces about one million tons of hornfels each year, much being used for ballast by both the Southern and Western Regions. The product is a metamorphosed sandstone which is very durable and particularly suited to today's high-speed railway. Nearing its destination on 18 July 1990 is No 33102 with the 9.38 from Tonbridge. *Peter Gray/DHM*

MELDON JUNCTION: After passing the quarry and crossing the West Okement Valley by way of the impressive 130-ft high Meldon Viaduct, the railway came to this junction. This appears to have been a rarely photographed location, possibly due to its fairly inaccessible position on an embankment. However, one way of recording it would have been from a passing train, such as this 5 March 1966 view from the front of the 10.05 am Okehampton–Bude DMU. By this time the up line had been taken out of use, but just visible on the right is the start of an up loop which ran to just short of the viaduct.

The North Cornwall route closed on 1 October 1966, with Meldon Quarry to Bere Alston following suit on 6 May 1968. Afterwards this stretch was converted into a road and used by lorries in connection with the building of a dam. This role completed, the formation is now slowly returning to nature, although some evidence of the temporary road surface remains in July 1990. *R. A. Lumber/DHM*

ASHBURY (FOR NORTH LEW) was the only crossing place between Meldon and Halwill after the closure of a loop at Maddaford Moor in 1919. Visible on the up platform on 16 May 1964 is the signal box of 1879 vintage, whilst the poster on the left-hand side of the single-storey station building is the Notice of Closure for the Bude and North Cornwall lines which had been issued two months earlier. 'N' Class 2-6-0 No 31849 is calling with the lightweight 3.11 pm Bude–Okehampton, a working which would probably have produced a 'T9' 4-4-0 until their final withdrawal from the area in 1961. The Maunsell-designed 'Ns' arrived locally in 1924 and for 40 years proved to be popular and successful engines.

The station buildings are now in residential use, with the platforms intact as part of the garden. Trees unfortunately obscure much of the July 1990 view. *R. A. Lumber/DHM*

HALWILL JUNCTION (1): The station was originally known as Halwill & Beaworthy, a station on the Devon & Cornwall Railway which commenced operations on 20 January 1879; it was renamed Halwill Junction in March 1887, just after the North Cornwall line to Launceston opened. A hamlet grew up around the station and retains the name to this day. By the time the rails from Torrington arrived in 1925, this was an important junction with the signal box holding four separate tablet machines for the four converging single lines. The station was renowned for its lengthy periods of calm which would be interrupted by great bursts of activity as trains would arrive in rapid succession from each direction, allowing connections or the exchange of portions. A typical such period is illustrated in this sequence of photos from 18 July 1964, with their present-day equivalents.

In the first view, Standard Class '4' 2-6-4T No 80037 is arriving with the 10.12 am Okehampton–Padstow/Bude. After the engine has departed for North Cornwall, sister loco No 80041 will take the rear portion forward to Bude. Meanwhile, No 80043 stands in the bay platform, having arrived with the 9.30 from Bude.

Work started in 1989 to develop a housing estate on the station site, and in this 17 July 1990 scene, only the background trees link the two pictures. *R. A. Lumber/DHM*

HALWILL JUNCTION (2): The opposite end of the station is pictured as 'West Country' 4-6-2 No 34020 *Seaton* enters with the 8.30 am Padstow–Waterloo, the house on the right being the obvious connection with the scene today. Obscured by the Bulleid 'Pacific' is the self-contained platform of the ND&CJLR which, together with its own run-round loop just down the line, allowed Torrington trains to be operated independently. *R. A. Lumber/DHM*

The final photograph is of 2-6-2T No 41249 arriving with the 8.52 from Torrington. In the background are the coaches from the 9.30 ex-Bude, which will be added to No 34020's load. *R. A. Lumber*

HOLSWORTHY was the terminus of the Devon & Cornwall Railway, but the LSWR subsequently extended the line some 19 miles to Bude in Cornwall, with services there commencing on 10 August 1898. An important livestock market operated here and cattle traffic was a valuable source of revenue for the railway, together with other agricultural produce. By the 1960s this had proved susceptible to road competition, and although there was still a healthy inwards traffic of coal and fertilisers, it was not enough to sustain freight services which were withdrawn from the area from 7 September 1964. Just prior to this, on 7 July, BR Class '4' 2-6-4T No 80042 stands in the station with the 11.45 Bude–Waterloo; the three through coaches will be added to the 11.00 ex-Padstow at Okehampton.

A proposal for withdrawing the passenger service from both Bude and Padstow had been submitted in March 1964, but objections led to a public enquiry. Eventually, after a lengthy wait, Ministerial consent was given to closure and the final trains ran on 1 October 1966. The station site was sold for commercial use and the main building is still standing. The trackbed has been filled in to platform level, but the edging slabs are still in evidence in July 1990. *R. A. Lumber/DHM*

ASHWATER was the first station on the North Cornwall Railway, which opened for traffic between Halwill and Launceston on 21 July 1886, with completion to Padstow on 27 March 1899. Pictured on 11 July 1964, during the last summer of through workings, the token is offered to the driver of 'Battle of Britain' 4-6-2 No 34066 *Spitfire* as it storms through with the 11.00 am Padstow–Waterloo. The WR had assumed control of all the SR lines west of Salisbury from 1 January 1963 and had announced its policy of making the Paddington route the main one for services to the South West. From September 1964 the Waterloo route was downgraded, with a 'Warship'-hauled semi-fast service terminating in Exeter.

The station building is now a private house, as pictured on 18 July 1990. The area beneath the bridge has been filled in and the road widened, thus producing a slightly different view today. *R. A. Lumber/DHM*

BRIDESTOWE opened on 12 October 1874 when the Devon & Cornwall Railway was extended to Lydford. It was located about 1¹/₂ miles up a steep road from the village, and was renowned for the large number of rabbits that were dispatched by passenger train, there being a good deal of warrening on nearby Dartmoor. For over 40 years until its closure in 1925, it was also the starting point for a 7-mile standard gauge railway running to the remote Rattlebrook Peatworks. The station closed to goods traffic on 5 June 1961, with passenger services ending on 6 May 1968. At 18.35 on the latter date, an Exeter to Plymouth DMU slowly moves away from the down platform.

The substantial station house is now occupied privately and, although the trackbed has been infilled to platform level, the down-side shelter, goods shed and concrete footbridge all survive. *R. A. Lumber/DHM*

LYDFORD was first reached by rail when the South Devon extended its Tavistock branch by some 19 miles to Launceston, with opening on 1 June 1865. In 1874 the LSWR route from Okehampton arrived and two years later that company gained access to Plymouth when a third track was added to the original line. Eventually the Plymouth, Devonport & South Western Junction Railway opened its Lydford to Devonport route on 2 June 1890, and the LSWR was then able to run independently from its rival. This complex history endowed Lydford with a fascinating layout, the two companies' stations being side by side with the centre platform shared. The Launceston branch closed to passengers on 31 December 1962, but sections were retained for goods. Lydford to Launceston closed entirely on 28 February 1966 and the track had been lifted by 27 April 1968, when we can see the 16.38 Plymouth–Exeter accelerating away from the station. The storage sidings on the left dated from the Second World War and the bombing of Plymouth. Today this area is occupied by a Riding Academy, with the trackbed becoming steadily more overgrown. *R. A. Lumber/DHM*

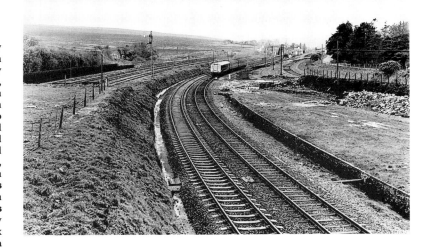

An Exeter–Plymouth train is photographed from the station footbridge, also on 27 April 1968. On the left is the joint signal box, opened in January 1917 to replace separate GWR and LSWR structures. *R. A. Lumber*

BERE ALSTON became a junction station on 2 March 1908 for the Callington branch, much of which had its origins in the 3 ft 6 in gauge East Cornwall Mineral Railway. Branch trains used the outer face of the up island platform and '02' 0-4-4T No 30193 of Friary shed is recorded on a Callington train on 28 March 1959.

The same view on 18 July 1990 is one of dereliction, but by looking to the right, as in the third photograph, there is a far happier scene as Class '108' DMU No 954 awaits departure after reversal with the 12.00 Plymouth–Gunnislake. The 5 miles of the branch beyond Gunnislake closed in 1966, with the final trains on the main line north to Meldon running on 4 May 1968. The remnants of these routes provide a valuable service to a geographically remote area which has poor road access to Plymouth. *Terry Nicholls/DHM*

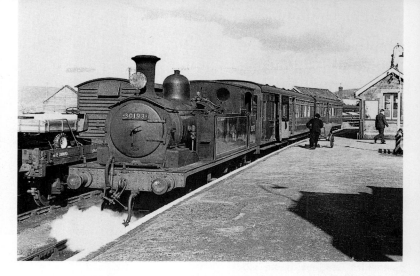

92

South Devon

EXMINSTER station possessed two island platforms and a number of sidings on the down side that were used in summer months to store coaches used for weekend holiday trains. It was opened to passengers in 1852, with closure from 30 March 1964. The final train, the 6.22 pm departure to Exeter St Davids, ran two days before and is pictured as the last two travellers board, while witnessing the event from the platform is local railway historian/publisher David St John Thomas.

Today no trace of the platforms remains as the trains speed by, such as on 1 April 1990 when Class '47' No 47824, appropriately named *Glorious Devon*, heads for Paddington with the 14.25 from Plymouth. The decaying signal box closed on 15 November 1986, whilst, after standing derelict for many years, the station building is in course of conversion to a restaurant. *R. A. Lumber/DHM*

DAWLISH WARREN possessed a beach but little else until the GWR opened a halt in 1905 to cater for daytrippers. In 1912 a new station was opened a little way to the north of the halt, and this remains open to serve the holiday centre that has grown around it. On 23 August 1975, Class '47' No 47152 heads Class '46' No 46047 along the down through road with the 08.45 Liverpool–Penzance; the 'Peak' had failed at Taunton and the train was running 56 minutes late.

Dawlish Warren signal box closed on 15 November 1986, but the building was retained pending possible conversion into a holiday flat. With the failure of this project, the structure was demolished in May 1990. Shortly afterwards, on 2 July, Class '47' No 47814 is pictured whilst working the 09.00 Aberdeen–Plymouth. *John Medley/DHM*

DAWLISH station is located on that famous stretch of railway known as the 'sea wall', a scenic route just over 4 miles long running from Dawlish Warren to Teignmouth. The line has captured the imagination of generations of holidaymakers in the summer months, but in winter it can be a different story as it is also susceptible to storm damage. Since the signalling came under the control of the Exeter panel, reversible working is possible over the up line in an attempt to mitigate the effects of such damage in the future.

On 24 April 1965, Class '22' No D6330 stands in the goods yard with an engineers' train. The yard closed soon after (17 May), and the site is now a car park, as illustrated on 17 July 1990 as 'Sprinter' No 155326 calls with the 9.30 Bristol Temple Meads–Paignton. *Geoff Lendon/DHM*

NEWTON ABBOT (1): This location was reached by the South Devon in December 1846. The company subsequently based its works and main locomotive depot here, and this decision did much to promote the development and future prosperity of the town. The station was reconstructed during the period 1925-7 at a cost of £140,000, and featured two long island platforms and a layout which remained substantially the same for 60 years. At the east end, on 31 March 1956, 2-6-0 No 6322 and 'Hall' No 4999 *Gopsal Hall* are pictured leaving with the Kensington Milk, whilst in the background Standard Class '3' 2-6-2T No 82005 approaches with a Goodrington–Hackney Yard goods. The photographer is standing on the detached bay platform used by Moretonhampstead trains.

The station's two mechanical signal boxes closed on 2 May 1987, and amongst the associated work only three platform faces remain with the up through and main lines taken out of use. The latter-day view shows the rationalisation on 17 July 1990 as two HST units await departure. *Peter Gray/DHM*

NEWTON ABBOT (2): The West box is illustrated on 25 April 1987 as Class '142' No 142026 arrives with the 11.24 from Paignton. One of the island platforms had already been shortened by then, but comparison with the modern scene on 3 July 1990 shows how much has changed in the most recent pair of photos in this book. Visible in the background is the closed diesel depot which had been built on the site of the steam shed, whilst the former wagon works on the right is now occupied by the publishers David & Charles.

There is some irony in the diesel units depicted, as the past view shows one of the 13 chocolate-and-cream liveried 'Skippers', allocated when new in 1985 to Laira TMD for local services. Due to technical problems, particularly associated with the gradients and curvature of the Cornish branches, they were transferred north by the end of 1987, to be replaced by a motley collection of first-generation units such as Metro-Cammell Class '101' No 829, which is working the 17.45 Exmouth–Paignton. *Both DHM*

HEATHFIELD (1): Opened as Chudleigh Road, the station was on the broad gauge Moretonhampstead branch which commenced operations on 4 July 1866. Part of this line followed the route of the Hay Tor Tramway, Devon's first railway, which had been built with granite track. Heathfield became a junction on 9 October 1882 when the first section of the standard gauge Teign Valley line was opened to Ashton. This line was to remain isolated until the gauge conversion in May 1892. The station is pictured on 7 August 1957 as 0-6-0PT No 7716 awaits departure with an Exeter train. The line on the left led to a brick and tile works.

After Moretonhampstead branch passenger services ended, the route survived for goods traffic until 6 April 1964 when the line was truncated at Bovey. In 1965 a new terminal was established about 1/2 mile from Heathfield and this currently receives one or two Gulf oil trains from Waterston each week, and the station loop has been retained for run-round purposes. Returning from the terminal on 16 September 1990 is Class '50' No 50031 *Hood* with Pathfinder Tours' 'The Taw Retour'. No 50032 *Courageous* is at the far end of the train. *R. A. Lumber/DHM*

TORQUAY: The Dartmouth & Torbay Railway opened from Torre (see page 6) to Paignton on 2 August 1859, its arrival helping to accelerate Torquay's growth, especially as a winter resort frequented by the wealthy. By the 1890s the type of visitor was changing and subsequently the town developed as a summer destination for the middle and working classes. Many of these visitors came by rail and this traffic reached its peak in the 1950s when the volume of trains would fully stretch resources. It was not unusual to see freight engines used, such as in this 3 September 1960 scene of Standard '9F' 2-10-0 No 92218 on the 9.55 Swansea–Kingswear.

Summer weekends still enliven activity on 'The Branch', but during weekdays there is only a limited through train service, and most long-distance travellers have to make connections at Newton Abbot using local trains such as the 14.45 Exmouth–Paignton, which on 19 July 1990 comprised Class '108' No 828. *Peter Gray/DHM*

CHURSTON was known as Brixham Road on the opening of the Dartmouth & Torbay from Paignton on 14 March 1861, but gained its later name when the Brixham branch opened on 28 February 1868. A further extension took the main route to Kingswear in 1864 with a steam ferry connection to a 'station' at Dartmouth. In a busy scene timed at 3.38 pm on 7 July 1956, the Brixham 'auto' stands in the bay platform with 0-4-2T No 1472 in charge, whilst the crew of 4-6-0 No 4973 *Sweeney Hall* await receipt of the token before departing with the 3.20 pm Kingswear–Cardiff. The 10.20 am Paddington–Kingswear is in the down platform behind 4-6-0 No 4082 *Windsor Castle*.

The last train to Brixham ran on 11 May 1963, whilst Churston's signal box closed on 20 October 1968 when the main line was singled. The rationalised scene is shown in July 1971 as Class '52' No D1023 *Western Fusilier* pauses with a Kingswear to Paddington train. On withdrawal in 1977, this loco was taken into the National Collection, and has since spent the majority of its preserved life back on this line, unfortunately without seeing much use. *Peter Gray/John Medley*

A view of the same location on 19 July 1990 presents a happier picture as 2-6-2T No 4588 draws away with the 17.00 Kingswear–Paignton. This stretch of railway was sold by BR in 1972 to the Dart Valley company and now operates as the Torbay & Dartmouth Steam Railway. The loop has been reinstated, although signalled with colour lights rather than semaphores, and the area to the right has been cleared for a new shed. *DHM*

105

DAINTON: Part of the legacy of Brunel's 'atmospheric caper' are the notorious South Devon banks, the engineer having believed that without the use of locomotives he could economise by reducing the radius of curves and also increase some gradients. Foremost among these inclines is the climb to Dainton which starts from Aller Junction, and where the final section up to Dainton Tunnel is at 1 in 37. On the other side of the tunnel, on 29 July 1959, 'Hall' 4-6-0 No 6941 *Fillongley Hall* passes Dainton Sidings signal box with the 10.45 Plymouth–Goodrington. On the left, banking engine 2-6-2T No 4174 awaits a path back to Aller.

The box closed on 14 February 1965, when a new Dainton Tunnel box opened a few yards nearer the camera. However, it too closed in 1987, and little evidence remains on 21 July 1990 as an HST unit forming the 9.40 Newquay–Glasgow Queen St passes, with power cars Nos 43021 and 43185 at either end. *Peter Gray/DHM*

TOTNES was reached by the South Devon Railway on 20 July 1847 and became a junction when the Ashburton line opened on 1 May 1872. Branch trains did not have their own facilities, but instead used the main platforms as illustrated on 25 October 1958 as 0-4-2T No 1470 moves its coach into position on the up side after taking water. Passenger services to Ashburton ended a few days later on 1 November. Pictured on the right is the two-road timber goods shed which was demolished in 1965.

The station is still open to passengers, and serves as a railhead for much of South Devon. Departing on 21 July 1990 is the 8.46 Penzance–Paddington HST. This platform was used by Dart Valley steam trains from 1985-9, but the company do not now consider that the cost of this facility is justified. *Peter Gray/DHM*

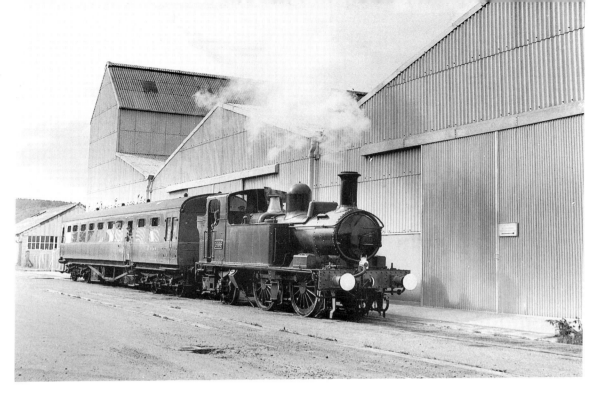

TOTNES QUAY: This line opened on 10 November 1873 when all trains were worked by horses. By the following year locos were permitted over part of the route, but horses were in control over the remainder until they were replaced by tractors from 1948. The branch was only $^3/_4$ mile long but served several industries along its way and trains continued until 1967. By then, other developments had taken place which would give the line a degree of glory, for in 1964 it became a storage site for the embryo Great Western Society, which at that time was also involved in the Dart Valley project. The two bodies were eventually to go their own ways, but during the brief period of occupation several steamings and open days were organised, such as on 26 June 1965 when 0-4-2T No 1466 and auto-trailer No W231W were in action.

Most of the stock departed from the site on 1 December 1967, with official closure of the line following, but GWR 0-6-0ST No 1363 remained until May 1969 and track lifting commenced later the same year. *Geoff Lendon/DHM*

BUCKFASTLEIGH station is pictured on 8 September 1962 after 2-6-2T No 4567 had arrived with the Plymouth Railway Circle's brake-van tour. At the time it was thought that this would be the last train over the line, as the final goods had run the previous day behind No 4555. However, within months of closure plans were announced for the purchase of the branch, and eventually services re-commenced on 5 April 1969 under the auspices of the Dart Valley Railway Company.

The station is now the furthest extent of operations, as unfortunately the trackbed from here to Ashburton has been buried beneath the A38 dual carriageway. On 20 July 1990, 0-6-0PT No 6435 is shown running round after arrival with the 16.05 from Littlehempston. The goods shed is now used as a museum, whilst the railway's works and servicing facilities are just to the left of this view. *R. A. Lumber/DHM*

BRENT station opened in 1848, but much alteration took place in 1893 when both the main line was doubled and the Kingsbridge branch was opened. The location presents an attractive scene on 21 May 1956 as 4-6-0 No 7820 *Dinmore Manor* departs with an up stopper, whilst 2-6-2T No 5533 stands at the island platform with a branch train.

The station closed in 1964 but the same viewpoint on 20 July 1990 shows that both the goods shed and signal box still stand, the former occupied by a furniture manufacturer and the latter used by permanent way staff. Class '47' No 47557 passes with the four vans comprising the 14.26 Plymouth–Newcastle parcels. *Peter Gray/DHM*

LODDISWELL was one of the three intermediate stations on the Kingsbridge branch, opened by the GWR on 19 December 1893. The station was built on a site partly cut out of the hillside bordering the Avon Valley, with the village a mile away on the opposite hillside. Its attractive location was ideal for camping coaches and these were introduced in 1934. After Nationalisation, old 'Toplight' vehicles were used, and two are visible as 2-6-2T No 4561 leaves on the 11.00 am Kingsbridge–Brent.

The same viewpoint today is obscured by the foliage which covers the formation, so a slightly different angle has been selected to show the station nestling amongst the trees. It is occupied as a private house with the canopy happily restored. To the left is the former Station Master's house. *Peter Gray/DHM*

KINGSBRIDGE station is shown to advantage in this fascinating scene on 5 March 1960 as small 'Prairie' tank No 4561 awaits departure with the 4.05 pm to Brent. Close study reveals the goods yard crane, with a concrete animal feed store and a corrugated iron carriage shed standing just to the right. The latter building was capable of holding two coaches, and also acted as a waiting room for connecting bus passengers. On the extreme right is the single-road engine shed which accommodated one tank loco, and was reached by a spur from the bay platform road.

The last trains ran on 14 September 1963 and the site has since been developed as a small industrial estate. A similar view today is meaningless due to a combination of dense undergrowth and the erection of a large building occupied by a coach firm. A gap in the trees does, however, allow this 12 July 1990 view of the main station building which has been extended by enclosing the area under the canopy. *Peter Gray/DHM*

Rails around Plymouth

INGRA TOR HALT on the Princetown branch was opened on 2 March 1936 in an attempt to counter road competition. The line had opened on 11 August 1883, although much of the circuitous route followed the earlier horse-drawn Plymouth & Dartmoor Railway. Amongst the goods carried by this mineral line had been granite from a quarry adjacent to the site of this halt. Traffic on the new branch was never heavy and there has to be some doubt whether it ever paid its way, although at one time it was used to transport prisoners to the infamous Princetown (Dartmoor) Prison. After Nationalisation, income dwindled further and closure came on 3 March 1956. On New Year's Eve 1955, 2-6-2T No 4568 draws the single-coach 4.00 pm from Princetown into the halt where it will collect a small band of enthusiasts.

The present picture was taken on 20 July 1990 and entailed a walk over the Moor and along part of the trackbed. During the course of this the photographer was reminded of the warning notice which once stood at this remote spot advising passengers to keep dogs on a lead because of the presence of snakes! *Peter Gray/DHM*

MARY TAVY & BLACKDOWN opened to passengers on 1 July 1865 when the Tavistock to Launceston line commenced operations. Built with two platforms, trains crossed frequently between 1876 and 1890 when LSWR trains travelled over the mixed gauge route between Lydford and Tavistock. On the opening of the Plymouth, Devonport & South Western Junction line in 1890, the loop was taken out of use and the down side closed. The signal box also closed at a later date and the solitary siding was controlled by a ground frame, until that was itself taken out of use in 1948. The station became an unstaffed halt from 11 August 1941, and is pictured on 23 September 1961 as 0-6-0PT No 4658 departs with a train from Launceston. The PD&SWJ route ran through the cutting just visible above the signal box.

The halt closed with the line on 31 December 1962. The former Station Master's house is a private residence; the platform still exists and can be located just behind the garden furniture in this July 1990 view. *Peter Gray/DHM*

LAIRA was the location for the main GWR engine shed in Plymouth. It opened in 1901 when the accommodation comprised a large roundhouse, but additional work in 1931 included an extension to the coal stage and the construction of a four-road straight shed. At Nationalisation there was an allocation of 104 locos, including 12 'Kings' which were employed on the main Paddington expresses. The 22 April 1962 view shows a variety of GWR 4-6-0s standing outside the 'new' shed. This building was used to house diesels pending completion of the new purpose-built depot nearby which opened at the end of 1962. The steam shed closed in May 1964, and the buildings were eventually demolished to make way for a staff car park and storage sidings, which are to the right of the July 1990 scene. *Terry Nicholls/DHM*

A view inside the roundhouse on 15 April 1962 shows 2-6-2T No 5572, 4-6-0 No 1003 *County of Wilts*, 'Modified Hall' 4-6-0 No 6988 *Swithland Hall*, 0-6-0PT No 4658, 2-6-2T No 4555 and 4-6-0 No 6938 *Corndean Hall*. Both 'Prairie' tanks are now preserved, by the GWS and DVR respectively. *Terry Nicholls*

LAIRA JUNCTION is illustrated on 1 December 1962 as '64XX' pannier tank No 6400 passes with a Tavistock train. The shed is visible in the background, whilst the line on the left formerly led to marshalling yards, but these had been closed in 1958 to allow the new diesel depot to be erected on the site. The signal box closed on 10 November 1973 when control passed to the Plymouth panel.

The modern view on 18 July 1990 includes Class '47' No 47825 *Thomas Telford* passing the same spot with the 10.00 Plymouth–Edinburgh. The sidings in the background form part of Laira TMD and inter alia are used as a dump for withdrawn locos. *Terry Nicholls/DHM*

PLYMOUTH FRIARY (1): Friary shed was opened in 1908, and was located about ¹/₂ mile east of the station and the site of an earlier depot. It comprised a long three-road through building with a lifting road along the south side, as illustrated with 'West Country' 4-6-2 No 34023 *Blackmore Vale* also in sight. This was one of two unrebuilt Bulleid 'Pacifics' to survive until the end of Southern Region steam in July 1967, and is now preserved on the Bluebell Railway.

The shed was transferred to the Western Region in 1958, but closed in May 1963 with the track being lifted the following year. A massive warehouse was built on the site, totally enclosing the area visible in the 'past' view.
Terry Nicholls/DHM

PLYMOUTH FRIARY (2): The station opened on 1 July 1891 when LSWR services were extended from North Road. In addition to main-line trains the platforms were subsequently to be used by Turnchapel and Yealmpton branch services. The station closed to passengers from 15 September 1958 when it was converted into Plymouth's main goods depot. Apart from the removal of the signalling the station is still largely intact in the 10 July 1965 view. However, the signal box and goods shed were demolished three months later, after which a new freight concentration building was erected. The station buildings were demolished in 1976. After a period as the main marshalling yard for the area, this role has now passed to Tavistock Junction and the 'new' building has been dismantled to make way for a DIY store which was under construction on 12 July 1990. *R. A. Lumber/DHM*

This 9 October 1969 photo recalls a busier period as Class '03' No D2140 indulges in shunting activity. This engine was withdrawn the following April and scrapped at Swindon Works. *R. A. Lumber*

TURNCHAPEL was the terminus of a short branch from Plymouth opened by the LSWR on 1 July 1897, and the line ran on beyond the station to wharves on the River Plym. These were taken over by the Admiralty during the First World War and became a long-standing source of traffic for the line. The expansion of Plymouth also promoted passenger services, but these were to suffer from road competition, and there was a steady decline until January 1951 when the branch was temporarily closed due to a severe coal shortage. Although a service was restored in the July, in the interim many passengers had transferred their allegiance to bus transport and final closure followed from 10 September 1951. Goods traffic survived another ten years, and several specials ran during this period, including this RCTS tour run as part of their Royal Albert Bridge centenary celebrations. Class '02' 0-4-4T No 30182 stands in the station with a LSWR gate-set on 2 May 1959.

After closure the station site was levelled and enclosed within the confines of an oil storage depot. All that remains to positively identify the location today is the fencing on top of the embankment. *Terry Nicholls/DHM*

YEALMPTON: The LSWR obtained an Act for the South Hams Railway which would leave the Turnchapel branch at Plymstock and go on to Modbury. The GWR feared that it would be extended to Torbay, and by a subsequent Act the rights to the Plymstock to Yealmpton part were transferred to that company, whilst the section on to Modbury was to be retained by the LSWR, each to have running powers over the other's track. The latter section was never built, but the GWR opened the Yealmpton Branch on 17 January 1898. Initially the line flourished with passenger trains running through to Millbay station, but the inevitable road competition resulted in early closure to passengers in 1930. Goods trains continued, and as part of the war effort passenger services were reinstated in 1941, this time to Friary, but only until final closure on 4 October 1947. The station is depicted when it was visited by a further RCTS special on 2 May 1959. The engine is 0-6-0PT No 6420 which is sandwiched between two pairs of auto-coaches.

The last goods ran on 26 February 1960 and there is little indication today that the station ever existed, as a housing estate was developed from 1972. In July 1990 only the trees on the skyline help to pinpoint the location.
Terry Nicholls/DHM

PLYMOUTH NORTH ROAD was a joint GWR/LSWR station, opened on 28 March 1877 when it was served by both companies' trains *en route* to their respective termini at Millbay and Devonport. After the opening of the Lydford to Devonport line in 1890, it became the terminus for LSWR services, but now down trains arrived from the west rather than the east. It lost some status when Friary opened, but gradually became the most important station in the city, particularly as through GWR services to Cornwall could operate without reversing in Millbay. The station was enlarged in both 1908 and 1939, and further remodelling occurred during 1959-62 when colour light signalling was also installed. Evidence of work in progress is provided in the 28 November 1959 scene as Laira's 'Castle' No 5069 *Isambard Kingdom Brunel* leaves with the 5.30 am Paddington–Penzance.

The same viewpoint on 23 September 1972 shows Class '42' No 824 *Highflyer* on 1B81 (despite the indicator panel), the 08.00 Bristol Temple Meads–Penzance. This was one of the last 'Warships' in service; all of the class were withdrawn by December of that year. *Peter Gray/John Medley*

In April 1974 a revised layout was introduced and these platforms no longer have through roads. Platform 3 is now the usual home for Gunnislake trains and on 12 July 1990 Class '101/108' hybrid unit No 862 awaits its 16.30 departure. *DHM*

MILLBAY opened on 2 April 1849 as the SDR's Plymouth terminus. The nearby docks were opened the following year and were connected by a short line running to the north of the station. Its importance diminished over the years and the station was closed to passengers from 23 April 1941 when its platforms were needed for goods traffic after the adjoining depot had been bombed. New carriage sidings were opened on the station site in 1959, and these are just discernible in the background on 21 April 1968, as Class '42' No D832 *Onslaught* heads for North Road with an ECS working. The roof on the left belongs to Harwell St Carriage Shed.

All track was taken out of use on 14 December 1969 apart from the docks lines, but these were also closed in June 1971. Today it is hard to believe that the railway ever existed. *R. A. Lumber/DHM*

DEVONPORT KINGS ROAD is illustrated on 15 August 1964 as Standard Class '5' 4-6-0 No 73044 prepares to leave with the 16.52 Plymouth–Eastleigh. The station dated from 18 May 1876 when it was the LSWR's terminus for trains travelling over the GWR route from Lydford. It became a through station when the Lydford to Devonport line opened on 2 June 1890, and the up and down lines were reversed. Closure came on 7 September 1964 when trains were diverted to the ex-GWR route to St Budeaux, but goods facilities were retained until 7 March 1971. The railway has now been erased from the landscape and the Plymouth College of Further Education built on the site. Only the retaining wall and houses on the left link these photographs. *R. A. Lumber/DHM*

INDEX OF LOCATIONS